Barn Owls

Nocturnal Hunters

Rebecca Rissman

raintree

Raintree is an imprint of Capstone Global Library Limited, a company incorporated in England and Wales having its registered office at 7 Pilgrim Street, London, EC4V 6LB – Registered company number: 6695582

www.raintreepublishers.co.uk
myorders@raintreepublishers.co.uk

Edited by Brynn Baker, Clare Lewis, and
    Helen Cox Cannons
Designed by Kyle Grenz and Tim Bond
Picture research by Tracy Cummins
Production by Helen McCreath
Originated by Capstone Global Library Limited
Printed and bound in China by Leo Paper Group

ISBN 978-1-406-28281-8 (hardback)
18 17 16 15 14
10 9 8 7 6 5 4 3 2 1

ISBN 978-1-406-28288-7 (paperback)
19 18 17 16 15
10 9 8 7 6 5 4 3 2 1

British Library Cataloguing in Publication Data
A full catalogue record for this book is available from the British Library.

Acknowledgements
We would like to thank the following for permission to reproduce photographs: FLPA: Derek Middleton, 7 mouse, Erica Olsen, 19, Gary K Smith, 21, Imagebroker, 5, 23d, Michael Durham/Minden Pictures, 7 bat, Paul Sawer, 17, Simon Litten, 20, 23c; Getty Images: Derrick Hamrick, 1, 23g, Oxford Scientific/Michael Leach, front cover; Science Source: Kenneth M. Highfill, 9; Shutterstock: Andrew Astbury, 7 fox, CreativeNature.nl, 10, Dr. Morley Read, 14, 15, 23e, Gerckens-Photo-Hamburg, 18, 23f, iceeyes198369, 6, Mark Bridger, 4, 23a, back cover, Miles Away Photography, 22, Stephen Mcsweeny, 12, Tom Reichner, 11, Piotr Krzeslak, 7 hedgehog; Superstock: imagebroker.net, 16, 23b.

Every effort has been made to contact copyright holders of material reproduced in this book. Any omissions will be rectified in subsequent printings if notice is given to the publisher.

All the Internet addresses (URLs) given in this book were valid at the time of going to press. However, due to the dynamic nature of the Internet, some addresses may have changed, or sites may have changed or ceased to exist since publication. While the author and publisher regret any inconvenience this may cause readers, no responsibility for any such changes can be accepted by either the author or the publisher.

Contents

What is a barn owl?

A barn owl is a large bird. Its body is covered in grey or brown feathers.

It has light-coloured feathers on its face.

A barn owl has sharp claws called talons. It has large eyes and a strong **beak**.

You rarely see barn owls during the day because they are **nocturnal**.

What does nocturnal mean?

Animals that are nocturnal are awake at night.

Nocturnal animals sleep during the day.

bat

fox

hedgehog

mouse

Many animals are nocturnal.

Bats, foxes, hedgehogs, and mice are nocturnal.

Where do barn owls live?

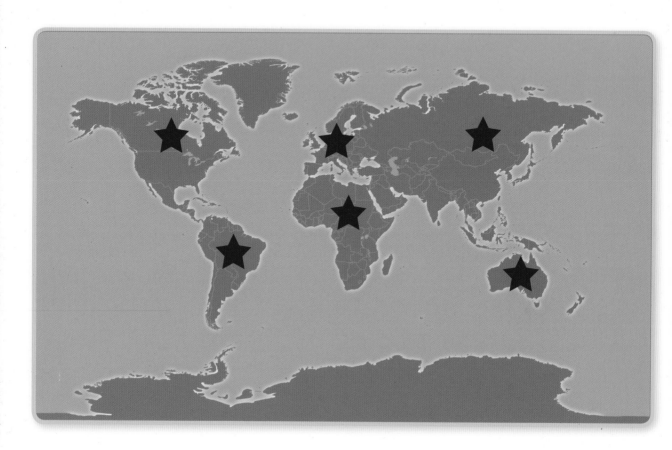

Barn owls live in Europe, North America, South America, Africa, Asia, and Australia.

They can live in forests, fields, deserts, farmlands, and even in cities.

Barn owls make nests in trees, caves, and buildings.

They are called barn owls because they often make nests in barns.

What do barn owls eat?

Barn owls hunt for nocturnal animals.

They usually eat small animals, such as mice and bats.

Some barn owls even eat larger animals, such as baby rabbits.

Barn owls also eat other small birds.

How do barn owls find prey?

Barn owls have very good hearing. They listen for **prey**.

Barn owls also have good eyesight. They can see small animals moving in the dark.

Barn owls fly quietly after prey.

They catch prey with their sharp talons.

What are owl pellets?

Owls often swallow their prey whole.

After they eat, they spit out **pellets**.

Pellets are the bones, fur, and feathers of owl prey.

Pellets show the different animals an owl has eaten.

What are baby barn owls like?

Female barn owls lay eggs in springtime.

Owl chicks are covered in **down** shortly after they hatch.

The mother owl brings prey back to the nest to feed the chicks.

Young owls leave the nest after two months.

Do barn owls have predators?

Barn owls have few **predators**.

In some places, raccoons, cats, and larger owls eat barn owl chicks.

Humans can harm barn owls too.

Growing cities and new buildings can make it hard for barn owls to find enough prey to eat.

How can you spot barn owls?

Barn owls are easiest to spot at **dusk**.
Watch for them swooping low over fields.

Owl droppings and pellets can tell you that a nest is nearby.

Listen for barn owl screeches. They can sometimes tell you where a nest is.

Barn owl body map

wing

beak

talon